D1278783

EUREKA!

It's an Airplane!

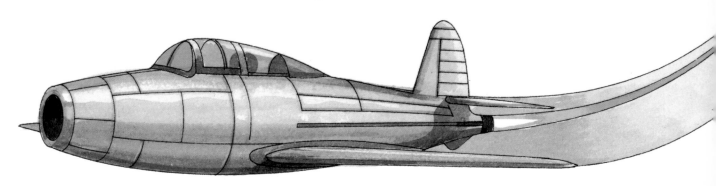

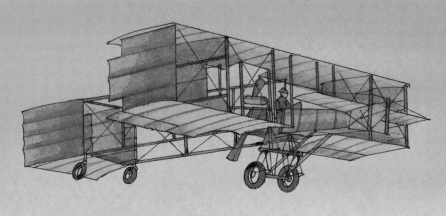

EUREKA!
It's an Airplane!

BY JEANNE BENDICK

*illustrations and
design by*
SAL MURDOCCA

The Millbrook Press • Brookfield, Connecticut

With special thanks to Wilson M. Hopkins, Jr.,
for his help and advice.

Note: Words that appear in *italic type* are
defined in the Glossary on page 46.

Library of Congress Cataloging-in-Publication Data
Bendick, Jeanne.
Eureka! It's an airplane! / by Jeanne Bendick
illustrated by Sal Murdocca.
p.   cm.—Inventing
Includes index.
Summary: Describes the development of the airplane and some of the
inventions that have made it a more common means of transportation.
ISBN 1-56294-058-9
1. Airplanes—Juvenile literature.   2. Aeronautics—History—
Juvenile literature.   3. Inventions—Juvenile literature.   [1.
Aeronautics—History.   2. Airplanes.   3. Inventions.]   I. Murdocca,
Sal, ill.   II. Title.   III. Series: Bendick, Jeanne. Inventing.
TL547.B379   1992
629.13'009—dc20   91-34791   CIP   AC

For Aunt Marcelle,
who flew on Monsieur Bleriot's lap
J.B.

For Nancy
S.M.

ARE YOU AN INVENTOR?

Inventing is thinking of ways to solve problems.

If you wanted to cross a stream in the woods, could you invent a bridge?

If you wanted to reach something on a high shelf, could you invent a ladder?

Could you invent a unit of measurement if you didn't have a ruler?

How many ways can you think of to fasten two pieces of cloth together?

How many ways can you think of to send a message to a friend?

Could you do all those things?

You're an inventor!

WHAT'S THAT FLYING THING?

IT'S A FLYING SHIP.

BUT IT HASN'T BEEN INVENTED YET.

NO, BUT IT WILL BE.

DISCOVERIES AND INVENTIONS

Many inventions depend on things people learn over time. One invention builds on another. A man named Hero, of Alexandria, Egypt, invented a steam reaction engine almost 2,000 years ago, but nobody knew how to put it to work. Later someone figured out that steam could move things. That discovery allowed someone else to invent a steam engine. Then still another person hitched that engine to a string of carriages. *Eureka!* A train! *Eureka* is a big word for inventors. It means "I have found it!" or "I've done it! Hooray!"

Many scientific discoveries are important to inventions that come much later. About 300 years ago Isaac Newton discovered the *Laws of Motion*, which explain how all things move. Every moving thing that was ever invented obeys these laws.

Law 1 says that if something isn't moving, it won't start moving by itself. And if something *is* moving, it won't stop or change direction unless something pushes against it.

Law 2 says that things move farther and faster when they are pushed harder. And they always move in the direction in which they are pushed or pulled unless something changes that direction.

Law 3 says that when something is pushed in one direction, there is always a *resistance* of the same size in the opposite direction.

The Laws of Motion help to explain how airplanes fly.

DREAMS OF FLYING

Some inventions, at first, are dreams of things that seem impossible, except to inventors. One dream was about flying. How could people fly?

Inventors imagined teams of birds pulling ships through the air.

They imagined flying carpets that were like place-to-place taxis.

They imagined people-wings, made of wax and feathers.

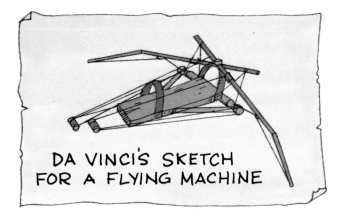

DA VINCI'S SKETCH FOR A FLYING MACHINE

In 1485 the artist and inventor Leonardo da Vinci drew a design for a machine he called an "ornithopter." Ornithopter means "bird winged." The ornithopter was supposed to be person-powered. Someone would wear the wings and fly by flapping them up and down. Over the years many inventors made wings and tried them out. They didn't work.

One reason was that nobody really understood how birds fly. It *looks* as if they fly by flapping their wings down and back, pushing themselves up and forward. That's not what happens.

The main parts of a bird's wings keep the bird up in the air. It's the feathers on the ends of the wings that push the bird forward as they twist backward when the wings flap down. You could call those feathers *propellers* and direction controls. A bird's wings keep it in the air, and those twisting feathers push it up, down, or forward.

In 1801, George Cayley, a British scientist, was one of the first to study how birds fly. He is called the father of *aerodynamics,* the study of how air moves around an object, whether the object is still, like a bridge, or moving, like a bird or an airplane. All airplane designers use aerodynamics when they design any kind of airplane.

HONK!

JOINT

IN 1804 CAYLEY MADE THIS AEROPLANE. IT WAS A KITE WING MOUNTED ON A POLE WITH A JOINTED TAIL UNIT.

HOW AIRPLANES FLY

Birds and airplanes are both heavier than air. It isn't easy to get an object that is heavier than air up into the air and flying. You can get a stone up into the air by throwing it. The harder you throw, the farther the stone will go in the direction in which you throw it (Newton's 2nd Law). But the stone won't fly. The force of *gravity* will pull it down.

(10)

A force is something that starts an object moving, or stops it, or changes its motion in some way. The force of gravity pulls everything on the Earth, or near it, toward the center of the Earth. We call that direction "down." There is no way to turn off gravity.

Another force pushes against everything on Earth that is moving, whether the object is a bird or an airplane in the air or a car or a person moving along the ground. That force is called *friction*. Friction pushes against moving objects until they stop (Newton's 1st Law). There is no way to turn off friction completely.

So how did inventors ever figure out a way to get an airplane up and keep it moving?

Can you think of any ways to beat the forces of gravity and friction?

How about using other forces?

The forces that get a plane up and keep it flying are called *thrust* and *lift*.

Thrust is the force of the engine, which moves the plane upward and forward faster than gravity and friction can drag it down. (Airplane designers call friction *"drag."*)

Lift is a force supplied by the air itself.

Air is a gas. Air is real. It presses against all sides of everything it touches: people, houses, mountains, clouds, airplanes. It never stops pressing.

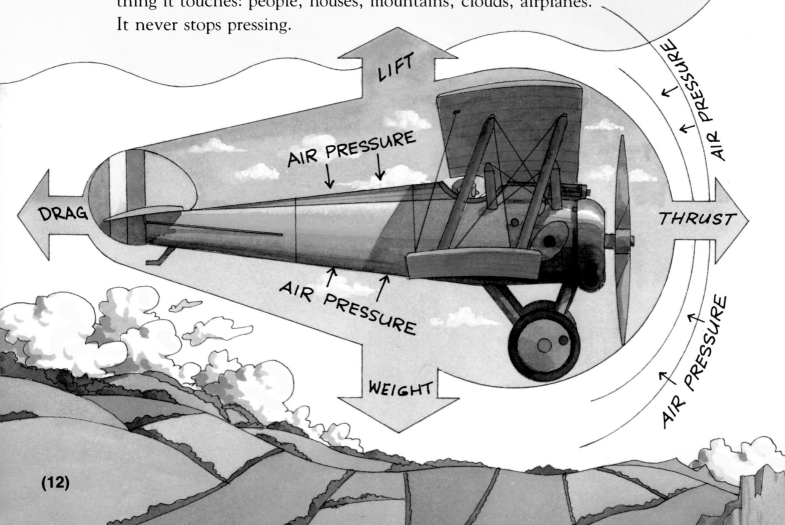

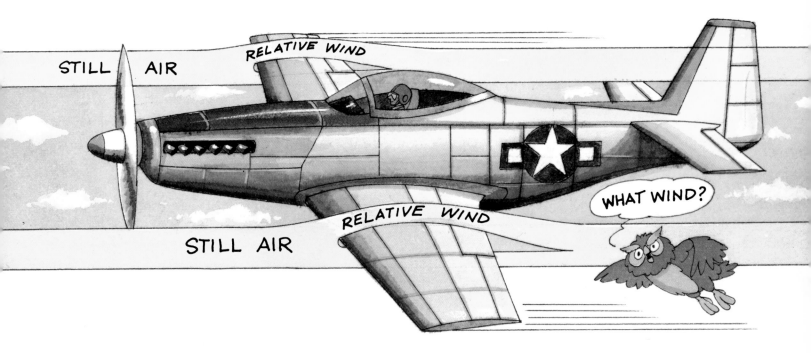

When thrust moves a plane forward through the air, the air around it seems to move back, over and under the plane's wings. Then the stream of air comes together again behind the plane. A moving car causes the same relative "wind."

More than 200 years ago Daniel Bernoulli, a Swiss scientist, discovered that the faster a gas, such as air, moves, the less it presses.

When air pressure is different in two places, the air with more pressure always moves toward the place where the air pressure is less.

Could you invent a way to make the air under a plane's wings press harder than the air on top of the wings? Could you invent a wing that would make the air underneath move more slowly than the air on top?

Hint: What would happen if you curved the top of the wing?

In 1901 two Americans, the Wright brothers, invented a wind tunnel and tested wings of different shapes. They found that if a wing is curved on top, the air moving across the top of the wing has to move faster, because it has to travel farther to meet the air that is moving past the straight wing bottom.

The slower-moving air under the wing presses harder, trying to move up to where the air is pressing less. It lifts the plane.

So four forces act on a plane when it is flying. Gravity pulls it down and drag holds it back. Thrust pushes it forward and lift pushes it up. For a plane to get into the air and keep flying, lift and thrust must exert more force than gravity and drag.

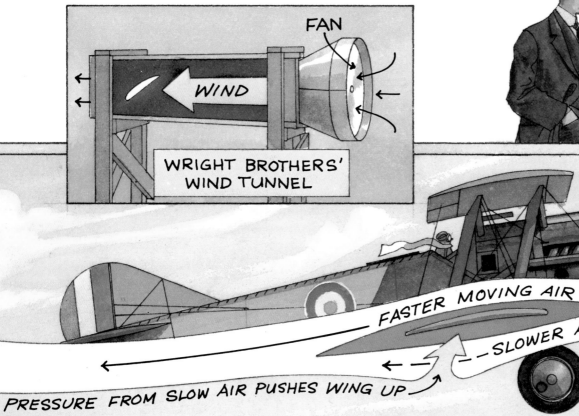

THE FIRST FLYING MACHINES

The very first flying machines were balloons.

Inventors notice things. More than 200 years ago two French brothers, Jacques and Joseph Montgolfier, noticed an interesting thing about smoke.

If you were watching a campfire, would you notice that smoke always rises? Would that give you an idea that maybe smoke could lift things?

Would that be the right idea?

How would you try to prove it? Would you try to lift something with smoke?

In 1783 the Montgolfiers made a huge bag and filled it with smoke from a fire. The bag lifted into the air. The brothers soon figured out that it wasn't the smoke that lifted their balloons, it was the hot air from the fire. Hot air rises because it is lighter than cooler air.

At first, nobody was very willing to try riding on hot air, so the first balloon passengers were a duck, a rooster, and a sheep, who couldn't object. They rode in a basket hanging under the balloon. Soon Montgolfier balloons were carrying human passengers, but balloons didn't satisfy inventors, who wanted more than to drift around the sky. They dreamed of flying from one place to another—fast. And they wanted wings.

The first aircraft with wings were *gliders*. In 1891 in Germany, an inventor named Otto Lilienthal built winged gliders. He built all kinds. Some had two sets of wings. Some had three sets, one above the other, like a three-layered cake. Lilienthal hung underneath his gliders. He held on with his hands and steered by swinging his legs and shifting his weight one way or the other.

There were many other glider fliers. They all knew hanging underneath was not a good idea. They all knew aircraft would need controls for steering and propellers to push or pull them through the air (Newton's 2nd Law). How could you supply power to the propeller?

You needed an engine. But in those days there were only steam engines, and they were too heavy.

In 1876 a German named Nikolaus August Otto invented the *internal-combustion engine*. An internal-combustion engine burns its fuel inside. Otto's first engine was big, noisy, and not very efficient. That means the engine used a lot of fuel to make a little power. It supplied more power than the heavier steam engine, but it still didn't do the job of pushing and lifting an airplane.

Nine years later Otto invented a more efficient engine.

And that's what the Wright brothers needed.

Wilbur and Orville Wright had been experimenting with gliders. They invented wings that gave them better control. They put *rudders* on the tails of their gliders so they could steer them.

They invented a new kind of propeller to push their plane.

Now they had an engine.

WRIGHT ENGINE

ENGINE TURNED TWO PROPELLERS

In December 1903, in Kitty Hawk, North Carolina, Orville Wright took off in *Flyer I*. (Orville and Wilbur tossed a coin to see which one would fly.)

Orville lay on the lower wing and steered with his hands and his feet. The plane was perched on a small truck that rolled down a rail until the truck and plane were going fast enough for the plane to lift off. *Flyer I* was in the air for 12 seconds and flew 120 feet (36 meters). (That's less than half the length of a modern passenger plane. But, *Eureka!*)

A few years later a Frenchman, Louis Bleriot, designed the first plane with single wings. He designed a new kind of propeller, for pulling the plane through the air. His plane had a tail with movable parts. In 1909, Bleriot flew his plane across the English Channel. Dreams of flying were coming true.

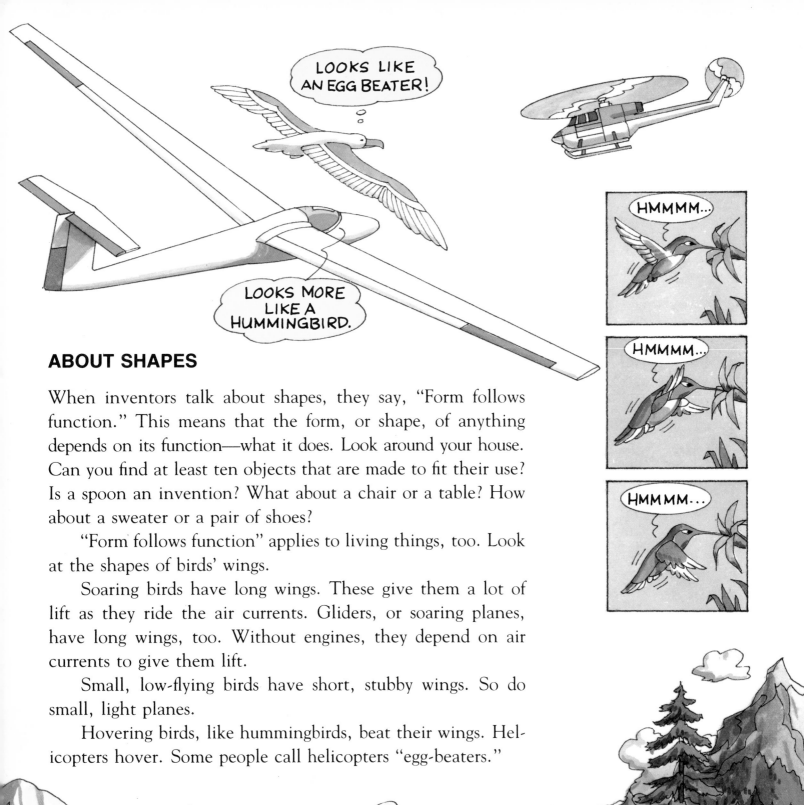

ABOUT SHAPES

When inventors talk about shapes, they say, "Form follows function." This means that the form, or shape, of anything depends on its function—what it does. Look around your house. Can you find at least ten objects that are made to fit their use? Is a spoon an invention? What about a chair or a table? How about a sweater or a pair of shoes?

"Form follows function" applies to living things, too. Look at the shapes of birds' wings.

Soaring birds have long wings. These give them a lot of lift as they ride the air currents. Gliders, or soaring planes, have long wings, too. Without engines, they depend on air currents to give them lift.

Small, low-flying birds have short, stubby wings. So do small, light planes.

Hovering birds, like hummingbirds, beat their wings. Helicopters hover. Some people call helicopters "egg-beaters."

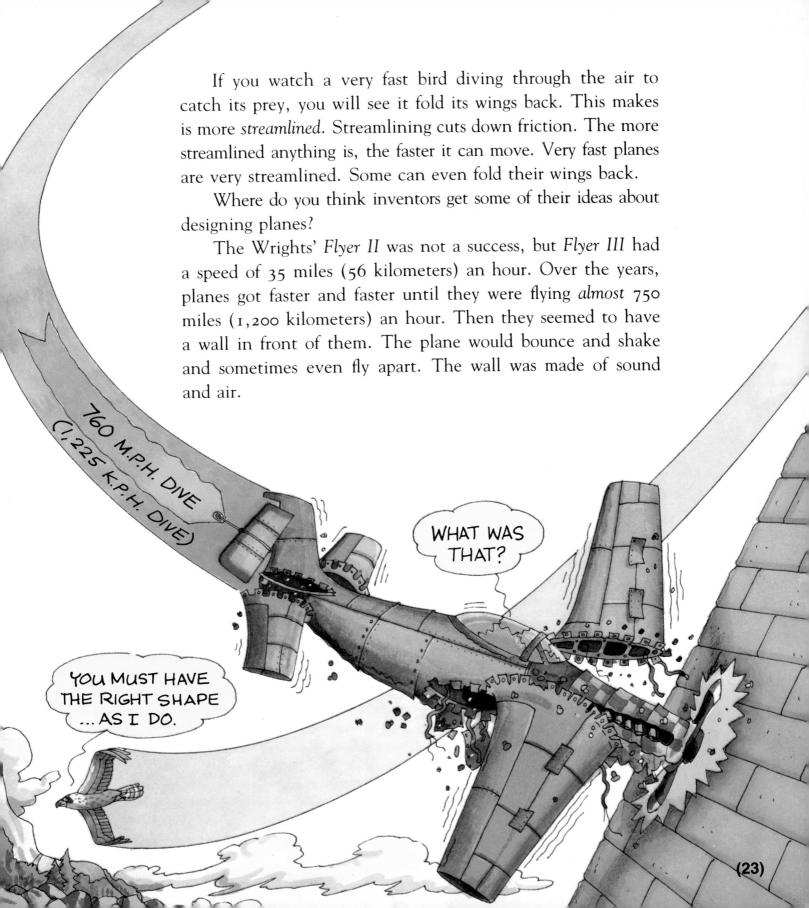

If you watch a very fast bird diving through the air to catch its prey, you will see it fold its wings back. This makes is more *streamlined*. Streamlining cuts down friction. The more streamlined anything is, the faster it can move. Very fast planes are very streamlined. Some can even fold their wings back.

Where do you think inventors get some of their ideas about designing planes?

The Wrights' *Flyer II* was not a success, but *Flyer III* had a speed of 35 miles (56 kilometers) an hour. Over the years, planes got faster and faster until they were flying *almost* 750 miles (1,200 kilometers) an hour. Then they seemed to have a wall in front of them. The plane would bounce and shake and sometimes even fly apart. The wall was made of sound and air.

760 M.P.H. DIVE (1,225 K.P.H. DIVE)

WHAT WAS THAT?

YOU MUST HAVE THE RIGHT SHAPE ...AS I DO.

It's hard to think of sound as being solid enough to make a wall that a plane couldn't pass through. You can't see sound or touch it. So what kind of a wall could that be? What is sound made of?

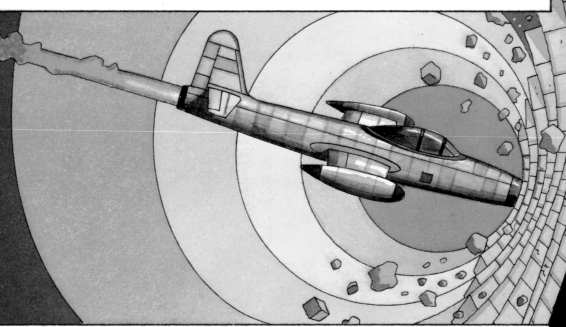

Sound is made when molecules of air jiggle and push together so they travel in little bunches called waves.

When you talk, sound waves travel away from you in all directions. When a plane flies, the sound of its engine travels away from it in all directions. Sound waves travel about 750 miles (1,200 kilometers) an hour. So if a plane is traveling slower than the speed of sound, it doesn't catch up with those waves of air. (Air is real, remember?) When a plane approaches the speed of sound, all those bunched-up waves can't get ahead of it. They pile up in front of the plane and stop it.

ON OCTOBER 3, 1967 THE X-15, A ROCKET PLANE, FLEW ALMOST SEVEN TIMES THE SPEED OF SOUND.

A SUPERSONIC JET AIRCRAFT

ON OCTOBER 14, 1947 THE BELL X-1 ROCKET PLANE WAS THE FIRST AIRCRAFT TO BREAK THROUGH THE SOUND BARRIER.

How do you think designers invented a plane that could slice through that *sound barrier?* Do you think they invented bigger, stronger engines? Or do you think they invented new airplane shapes? Think about the word "slice".

Designers thought up new shapes to help planes cut through the wall of sound. *Supersonic* means "faster than sound." Supersonic planes have long, sharp noses. Their wings sweep back. They are designed to slice through the wall of sound instead of banging into it.

(25)

HOW AIRPLANE ENGINES WORK

An airplane engine supplies the thrust that moves the plane through the air.

Some engines turn propellers. Another name for propeller is *airscrew,* because the propeller screws its way through the air, pulling the plane behind it.

Some small planes have *piston engines* that turn their propellers. A piston engine is an internal-combustion engine. It works like this:

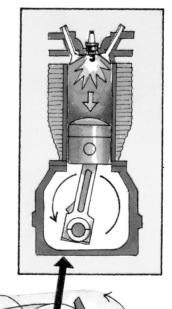

Many airplanes have turbojet engines. A *jet engine* is called a *reaction engine.* In a reaction engine, expanding hot gases push hard against the front of the engine. Then these gases bounce back and shoot out of the rear exhaust, pushing the plane forward (Isaac Newton's 3rd Law, remember?).

HOT AIR EXPANDS AND PUSHES OUT THE REAR

EXPANDED AIR RUSHES THROUGH TURBINES.

COMBUSTION CHAMBER

RUSHING EXHAUST PUSH JET FORWARD →

AIR FORWARD →

AIR

AIR

AIR IS COMPRESSED AND HEATED.

Some jet planes have *turbofan engines*.
They work like this:

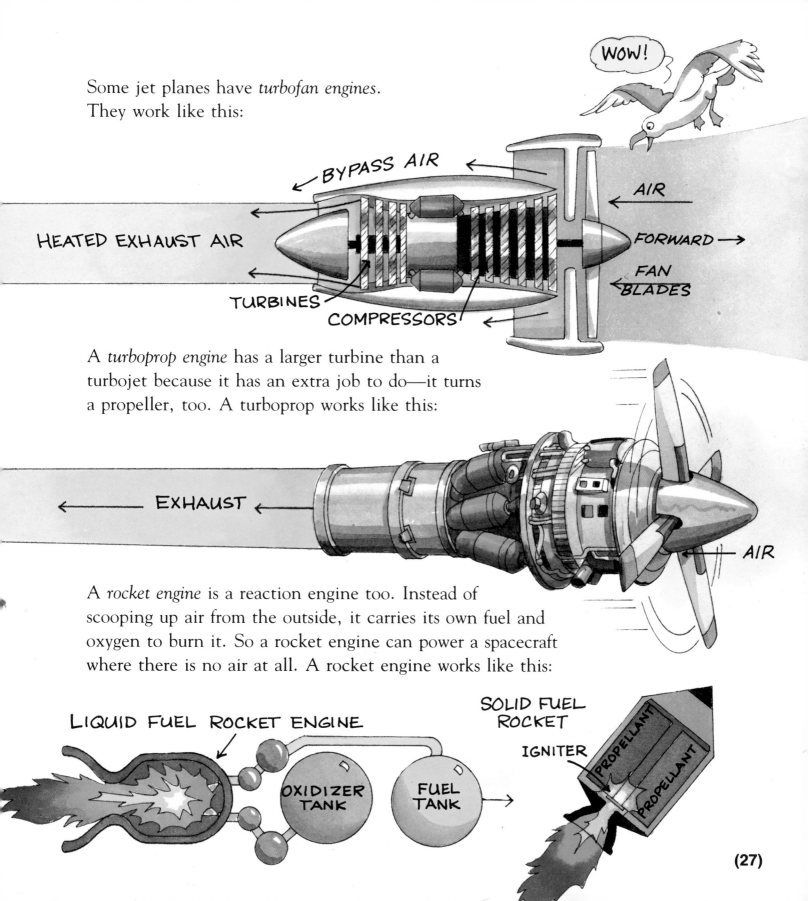

WOW!

BYPASS AIR

AIR

HEATED EXHAUST AIR

FORWARD

FAN BLADES

TURBINES

COMPRESSORS

A *turboprop engine* has a larger turbine than a turbojet because it has an extra job to do—it turns a propeller, too. A turboprop works like this:

EXHAUST

AIR

A *rocket engine* is a reaction engine too. Instead of scooping up air from the outside, it carries its own fuel and oxygen to burn it. So a rocket engine can power a spacecraft where there is no air at all. A rocket engine works like this:

LIQUID FUEL ROCKET ENGINE

OXIDIZER TANK

FUEL TANK

SOLID FUEL ROCKET

IGNITER

PROPELLANT

PROPELLANT

(27)

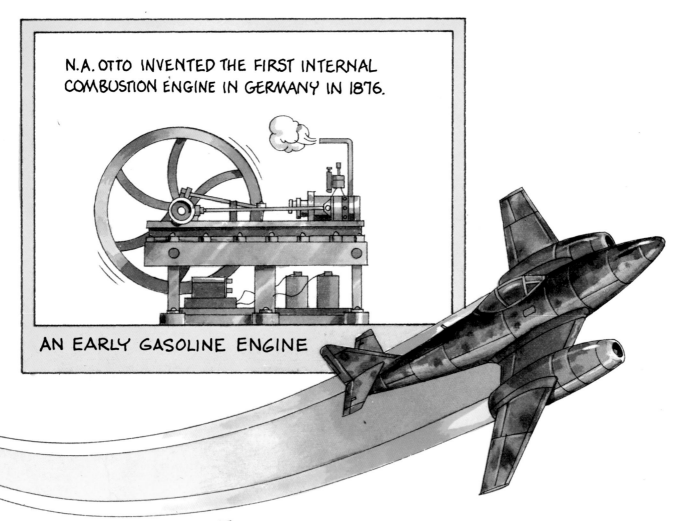

N.A. OTTO INVENTED THE FIRST INTERNAL COMBUSTION ENGINE IN GERMANY IN 1876.

AN EARLY GASOLINE ENGINE

THE FIRST TURBOJET AIRPLANE WAS FLOWN IN GERMANY IN 1939.

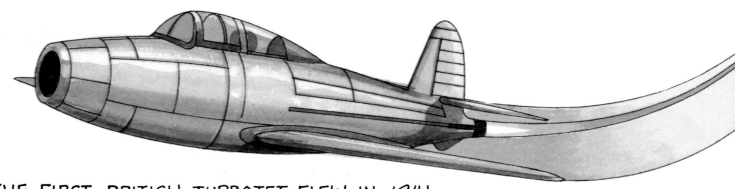

THE FIRST BRITISH TURBOJET FLEW IN 1941.

THE SOLID FUEL ROCKET WAS INVENTED BY THE CHINESE. IT WAS USED IN A BATTLE IN 1232.

ROBERT GODDARD, IN THE UNITED STATES, BUILT THE FIRST LIQUID FUEL ROCKET IN 1926.

PUTTING IT ALL TOGETHER

Now, inventor, at last you have a machine that flies.

It has a single set of wings and a metal skin. (Earlier planes were made of many layers of tulipwood, which were shaped, glued, and covered with fabric.)

You don't have to lie out flat on the lower wing any more. You have a seat built into the *fuselage*—the body of the plane. Your sitting place is called the *cockpit*.

The cockpits in today's big airplanes are called *flight decks*. There is room for pilots, crew, and sometimes hundreds of instruments and controls. Of course, you need only a dozen of those in your plane.

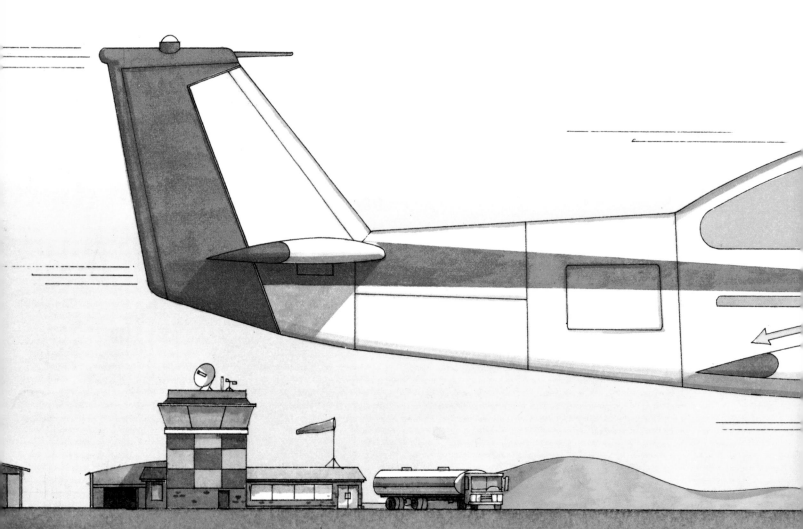

Now you're ready to take off. What's your first step up into the sky?

You start the engine. But you can't take off until enough air is moving over and under your wings to give them lift. To make a wind, you need to start rolling along the ground. Luckily, Monsieur Bleriot has put wheels on the plane. (And later, another inventor has made them retractable. They fold up into the plane when it is in the air. That reduces drag.)

You need speed along the ground. How do you make the engine go faster?

A handle called the *throttle* is connected to the plane's engine. The more the throttle is open, the more fuel goes into the engine, and the faster the engine goes, the faster the plane goes. You're *taxiing* and you're ready to take off.

FASTER AIR

SLOWER AIR

How do you do that?

You use your *controls.*

The *control surfaces* are the movable parts of a plane's wings and tail. The wings have hinged sections that move up and down. The tail of your plane has movable parts that pivot to help you change directions.

It wouldn't be handy to have separate controls for all those moving tail and wing sections—you'd have to have more arms than an octopus! Luckily, inventors have given you one control that's connected to control surfaces on the tail and wings.

DON'T PULL IT BACK TOO HARD!

AILERON

FLAPS ARE NOT CONTROLLED BY THE STICK.

FLAP

THIS IS THE STICK. WATCH!

ELEVATOR

RUDDER

ELEVATOR

THESE STABILIZERS DO NOT MOVE.

FLAP

FLAPS ARE USED FOR LANDING AND ONLY MOVE DOWN.

THE STICK CONTROLS BOTH AILERONS TOO. THEY MOVE UP AND DOWN.

It's called the *stick*.

The stick is connected to movable parts of the plane's tail, called *elevators*. Pulling the stick back makes the elevators go up. This makes the tail of the plane go down, which makes the nose of the plane go up. A plane follows its nose, so the plane climbs.

Pushing the stick forward makes the elevators go down. Then the tail goes up and the nose of the plane points toward the ground. And the plane follows its nose down.

What about the other directions?

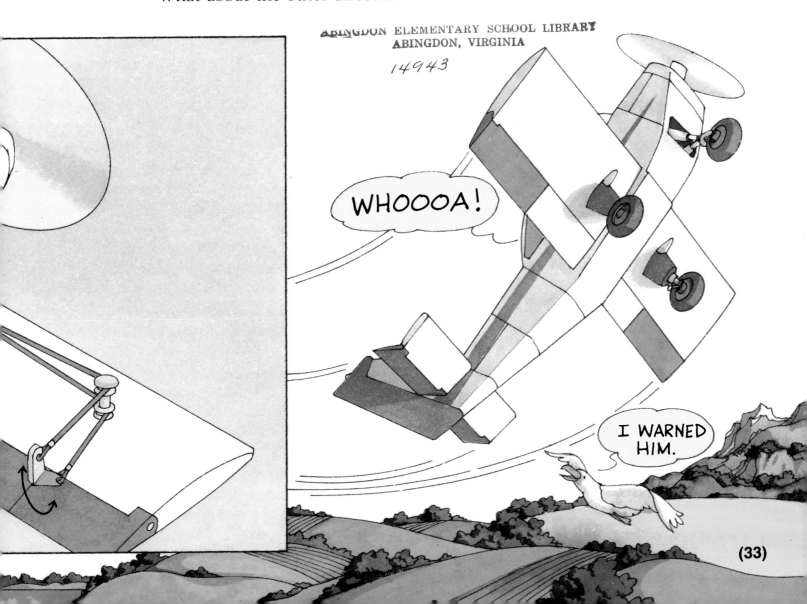

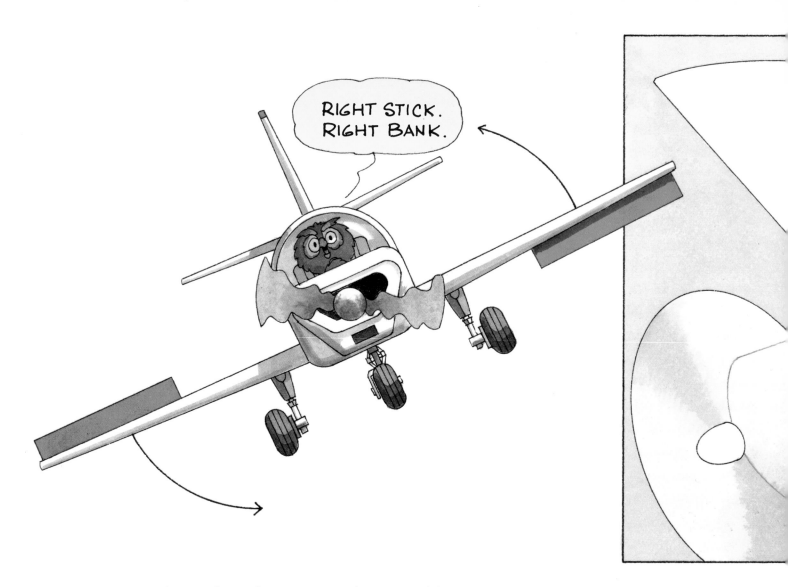

The stick is also connected to movable parts of the wings, which are called *ailerons*. Pushing the stick to the left or right makes the ailerons on one wing go down and the ailerons on the other wing go up. This makes the plane tip to the left or right. Fliers call this *banking* the plane. You must bank to turn.

How do you turn? So far you have pushed the stick forward and pulled it back. You have pushed it to the left and right. There are no other stick positions.

What about using your feet?

There are two pedals on the floor called *rudder pedals*. The pedals are connected to the hinged rudder on the plane's tail. Pushing on the left pedal makes the plane *yaw*, or swerve, to the left. Pushing on the right pedal makes the plane yaw to the right. Of course, being a good pilot, you use ailerons and rudder together.

IT HAD TO BE INVENTED

Suppose you are living at the start of the age of airplanes.

Inventing new and better planes would be important, but what are some of the other problems you have to solve?

Problem: Early planes rolled across bumpy fields before take-off. What could you invent that would make taking off and landing smoother?
Invention: How about a runway?

Problem: Planes should take off and land into the wind to give them more lift. Could you think of a way to show the pilots which way the wind is blowing?
Invention: How about inventing a wind sock?

Problem: How do you know in what direction you are flying? And which way do you have to go to get where you're going?

Invention: The *gyrocompass*. The first magnetic compass was invented by the Chinese in the 1100s. Now, pilots use a gyrocompass. The heart of a gyrocompass is a *gyroscope*. This does not bounce around like an ordinary magnetic compass and works better in the air.

The gyroscope was invented in France, by Jean Foucault, about 150 years ago. The gyrocompass was invented by Elmer Sperry and his son, also named Elmer, more than 50 years ago.

A GYROSCOPE ALWAYS STAYS IN A SET DIRECTION. THE AIRPLANE'S GYROCOMPASS IS FIXED ON NORTH.

Problem: How do you know when you're flying straight and level? If you are inside the clouds, you can't always tell if you're headed up or down, tilted, or even upside down. That could be dangerous.

Invention: Another gyroscope instrument shows you the horizon line so you can see how you are flying and what you need to do to get back to straight and level. The Sperrys invented that, too.

ARTIFICIAL HORIZON

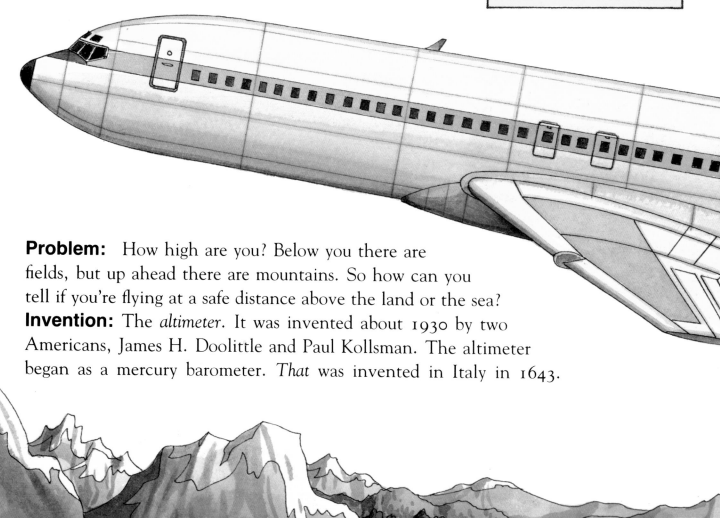

Problem: How high are you? Below you there are fields, but up ahead there are mountains. So how can you tell if you're flying at a safe distance above the land or the sea?

Invention: The *altimeter*. It was invented about 1930 by two Americans, James H. Doolittle and Paul Kollsman. The altimeter began as a mercury barometer. *That* was invented in Italy in 1643.

Problem: How fast are you going through the air? (That's what makes a plane fly!) *Airspeed* is different from *ground speed*. If the wind is blowing with you (a *tail wind*), it speeds you up, and if the wind is blowing against you (a *head wind*), it slows you down over the ground.

Invention: The *airspeed indicator*.
It was invented in France in 1910.

ALTIMETER

AIRSPEED INDICATOR

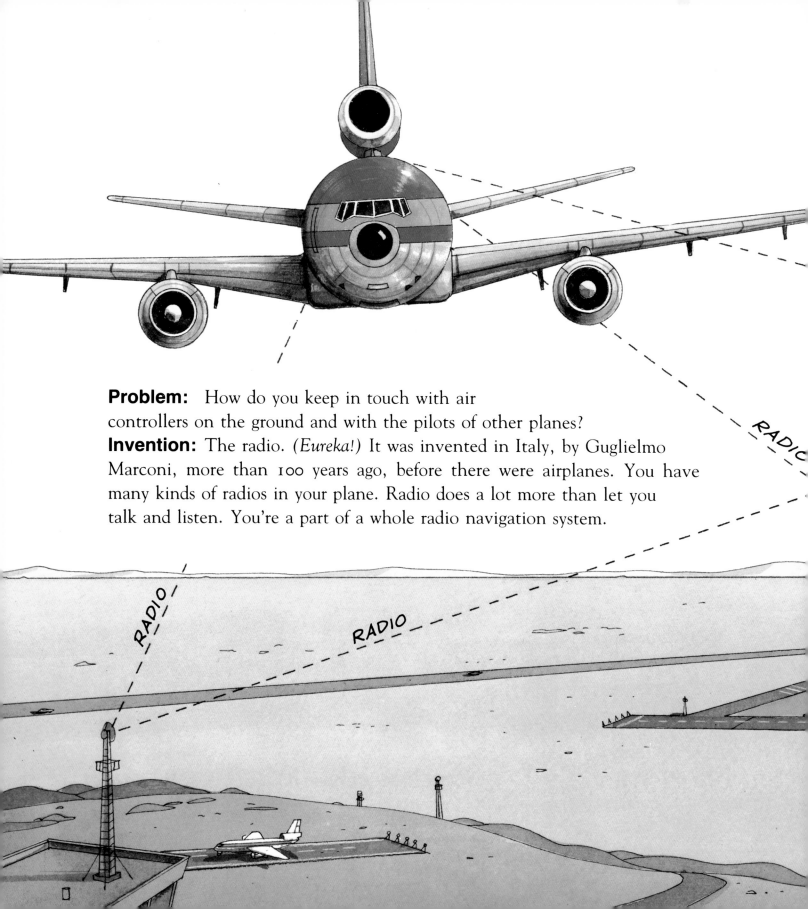

Problem: How do you keep in touch with air
controllers on the ground and with the pilots of other planes?
Invention: The radio. *(Eureka!)* It was invented in Italy, by Guglielmo
Marconi, more than 100 years ago, before there were airplanes. You have
many kinds of radios in your plane. Radio does a lot more than let you
talk and listen. You're a part of a whole radio navigation system.

Problem: How do you stay on course? There are no road maps or signposts in the sky.

Invention: Radio beacons on the ground send out radio waves that are received by an instrument in the plane. These show your road through the sky. A pointer on the instrument tells if you are off course and which way to turn to get back on. The system is called VOR (very-high-frequency omnirange).

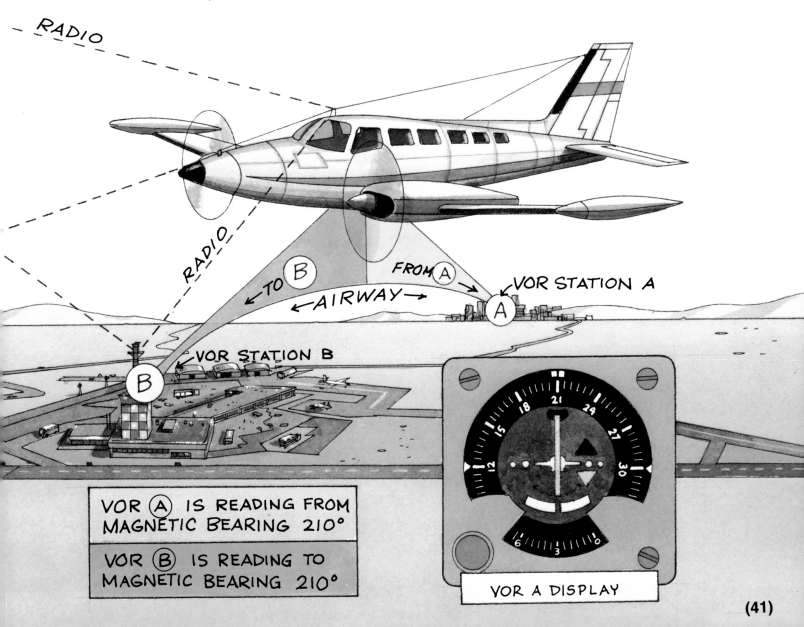

RADIO

RADIO

←TO Ⓑ

FROM Ⓐ

←AIRWAY→

VOR STATION A

Ⓐ

VOR STATION B

Ⓑ

VOR Ⓐ IS READING FROM MAGNETIC BEARING 210°

VOR Ⓑ IS READING TO MAGNETIC BEARING 210°

VOR A DISPLAY

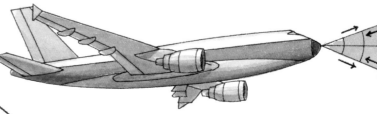
RADAR SIGNAL BOUNCES OFF CLOUDS BACK TO AIRCRAFT JUST LIKE AN ECHO.

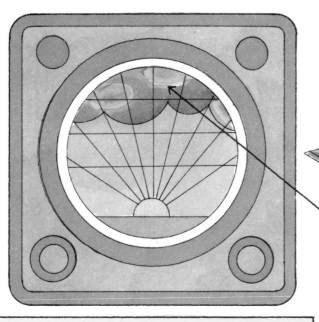

CLOUD SHAPE APPEARS ON RADAR SCREEN.

RADAR SCREEN ON AIRPLANE

Problem: How do you know if you are flying near other planes? How do you know if there are dangerous storms on your course, so you can avoid them? Could you invent something that warns you?

Invention: A radio that sends out signals in all directions. If the signals hit anything—a thunderhead, a mountain, another plane—they bounce back and make an image on a screen, showing where that object is. *Eureka!* What an invention! It's called *radar*. An American inventor, Nikola Tesla, had the first idea for radar in 1900. It was perfected in 1940.

ILS, OR INSTRUMENT LANDING SYSTEM

ILS PATH

ILS OUTER MARKER   ILS MIDDLE MARKER

Problem: Landing safely. Suppose the weather is bad. Suppose you can't even see the airport. How could you solve *that* problem?

Invention: An instrument landing system that guides your plane safely onto the airport runway on *automatic pilot*. You don't even have to touch the controls, except to lower the landing gear. (Another instrument shows you when the wheels are down.) James H. Doolittle, in 1929, was the first to use the instrument landing system he designed.

ILS GLIDE PATH   ILS LOCALIZER →

Problem: Hundreds of hungry people are flying on your airliner. How can you feed them all? There isn't room for a big kitchen in an airliner.

Invention: A movable pantry full of hot food that can be prepared somewhere else and lifted right into the plane before it takes off.

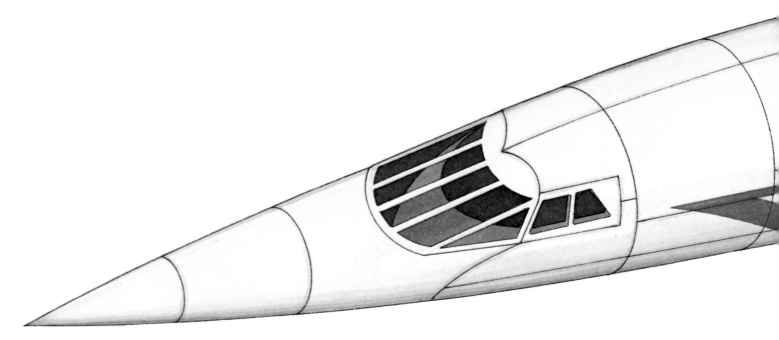

Problem: People need the amount of air pressure that is at or near sea level on Earth. And they need oxygen to breathe. But airliners fly at altitudes where the air is thin and there is not enough oxygen to breathe.

Invention: *Pressurizing* the cabin of the plane. Once the inside of the plane is airtight to the outside, air with oxygen, at ground-level pressure, is supplied to the cabin.

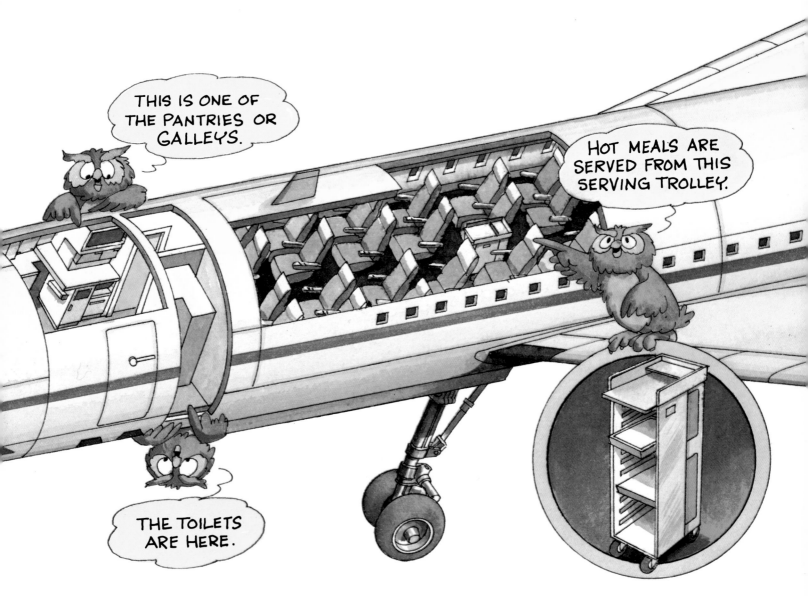

Problem: People need to go to the bathroom during a flight.
Invention: A chemical airplane toilet. Is that an important invention? *Eureka!* It certainly is.

What other inventions can you think of that solved flying problems? What still needs to be invented? What inventions can *you* think of for future flying?

GLOSSARY

Aerodynamics. The study of how air moves.

Ailerons. Surfaces in the wings that control banking for a turn.

Airscrew. The propeller.

Airspeed. How fast the plane is moving through the air.

Airspeed indicator. A device that shows how fast the plane is moving through the air.

Altimeter. Instrument that shows the height of a plane above sea level.

Automatic pilot. An instrument system that guides the plane without the pilot touching the controls.

Banking. Lowering a wing to make a turn.

Cockpit. Where the pilot sits.

Control Surfaces. The movable parts of a plane's wings and tail.

Controls. The throttle, the stick, and the rudder pedals.

Drag. The friction that pushes backward against a plane moving forward through the air.

Elevators. Tail control surfaces that cause a plane's nose to go up or down.

Eureka! A Greek word meaning, "I have found it!"

Flight deck. In a large plane, the compartment for crew and instruments.

Friction. A force that pushes against everything that is moving.

Fuselage. The body of a plane.

Glider. An airplane with no engine or propeller.

Gravity. The force that pulls everything on Earth toward the center of the planet.

Ground speed. How fast the plane is moving over the ground.

Gyrocompass. A special compass that shows the plane's direction.

Gyroscope. A device that always points to a set direction, no matter how the plane is moving.

Head wind. A wind blowing opposite to the direction of the flying plane.

Inertia. Resistance to a change of speed or direction.

Internal-combustion engine. An engine that burns its fuel internally.

Jet engine. A reaction engine that pushes a plane forward by forcing a blast of gases out of the rear.

Laws of Motion. Newton's three laws that explain how all things move.

Lift. The upward force from air moving under and over a plane's wings.

Piston engine. An internal-combustion engine that turns a propeller.

Pressurizing. Keeping air and oxygen pressure inside the plane the same as it is at sea level.

Propeller. A "screw" that pulls a plane through the air.

Radar. A radio signal that bounces from objects back to the source, where it makes an image on a screen.

Reaction engine. A jet or rocket engine that uses Newton's 3rd Law of Motion.

Resistance. A force that seems to push in the opposite direction against anything moving.

Rocket engine. A reaction engine that carries its own fuel and the oxygen to burn it.

Rudder. Tail control surface that makes the plane skid left or right.

Rudder pedals. The controls for the rudder.

Sound barrier. The wall of air in front of a plane as it approaches the speed of sound.

Stick. The lever a pilot uses to control the plane's elevators and ailerons.

Streamlined. Shaped to cut down the drag of air friction.

Supersonic. Faster than the speed of sound.

Tail wind. A wind that is blowing in the same direction as the flying plane.

Taxiing. Moving on the runway.

Throttle. Handle that controls how much fuel goes to the engine.

Thrust. The force that moves a plane forward.

Turbofan engine. A jet engine with long compressor blades that blow air back the way a propeller does.

Turboprop engine. A jet engine whose turbine also turns a propeller.

Yaw. To change direction.

INDEX